29 Things To Do

Ideas for an Effective Job Search

Rosemary Augustine

29 Things to Do ...
Ideas for an Effective Job Search
By Rosemary Augustine

© **2008 - 2013 Rosemary Augustine**

Electronic Versions: 2009, 2010, 2011, 2012, 2013

All Rights Reserved.

Published by:
Blue Spruce Publishing Company
750 Old Lancaster Road
Berwyn, PA 19312
info@BlueSprucePublishing.com
610.647.8863

Cover Photo: City Skyline - Original Acrylic
Painting by Rosemary Augustine

Author Photo: Elsie Koenig

ISBN-10: 0-9644711-0-8
ISBN-13: 978-0-9644711-0-8

DEDICATION

When I wrote my first book in 1995 called, *Facing Changes In Employment*, I dedicated the book to the memory of my father, Ernie Austin Augustine, who taught me the meaning of perseverance and the value of self-discipline. Those qualities are still relevant today, in any job search.

My father was passionate about music. And although he ran a business as the local dry cleaner in a small town, he played music from the time he was a teenager until a few days before he died. He understood networking before it became a popular term for an effective job search, and he valued connections, community and his family.

I continue to value the principals my father taught me, and know that although he has been gone 30+ years, his dedication to his passion is something each and every one of us should aspire to everyday. I dedicate this book to my father and to those who live and work their passion each and every day.

INTRODUCTION

When in a job search there are always things to do. However, we often get sidetracked and just sit and stare out the window. There are a lot of things we can do, like balance the checkbook or take a nap. But does it get us closer to a new position?

How do you motivate yourself? When you've sent the resumes and now you are playing the waiting game, what else is there? What can you do when you think you have nothing left to do?

Whether it takes you 15 minutes or all day, it's your choice. Here is a list of 29 things that will help you in your job search for those days when you think you have nothing left to do.

#1

Call a friend or associate to have coffee with, especially one that you haven't seen or spoken to recently. *This gives you a chance to catch up, network, and get some new ideas. It may also be an opportunity to learn of a few new contacts.*

29 Things To Do

#**2**

Have coffee by yourself at a specialty coffee shop. *Use this time to organize your week and review what you've accomplished so far. You may want to journal, bring your laptop and work, or just enjoy the taste of your coffee.*

#3

Listen to a motivational tape. *The 7 Habits of Highly Effective People is my favorite tape. Pick one up at the Library and listen to it while driving, or if you are taking 30 minutes to sort papers - just listen to the inspirational words.*

#4

Call your network of friends and give a status report. *Have a handful of people that you check in with on a regular basis to keep you accountable during your job search.*

#5

Call your agency network and get a status report. *When's the last time you called the list of recruiters you thought would find you a job? Check in with them and see what job orders they may be trying to fill.*

#6

Find a new company you've never contacted and call for an informational interview. *Brainstorm additional companies you are interested in. Who is the competition of the companies already on your target market list? Pick one and make a list of questions for your informational interview.*

#7

Read excerpts from an inspirational book. *Early in the morning, for a mid-afternoon pick up or before going to bed, read daily quotes for a spiritual pick up.*

#8

Re-write your goals and list 5 new ones. *In reviewing your goals, what ones have you achieved? What goals need to be re-evaluated? What are 5 new goals that can be added to your list? Include an approximate completion date to achieve the goals, i.e.: by June 15th; complete by 2014; complete in my lifetime.*

29 Things To Do

#9

Develop 3 new daily affirmations and incorporate them into your existing list of affirmations. *This takes some thinking – positive thinking. Update your affirmations, and/or create new ones to generate a positive inflow of energy.*

#10

Read the business section of the daily newspaper and find 2 new leads. *Read the paper from a different perspective or review sections you never read and see what new things you find.*

#11

Locate a new contact for job referrals. *Who in your network have you not contacted yet for information, ideas and/or job leads? Identify that person and give them a call today.*

#12

Critique your last interview: list 5 things you did right and 3 things to do differently next time. *This is a time for constructive feedback, not a time to beat yourself up over an interview. At least you can prepare for future interviews and practice, practice, practice before you head out to the next one.*

#13

Schedule or attend a new exercise class. *What's your favorite exercise? A spinning class? Walking on the treadmill? Yoga? Consider going as a guest to a friend's health club. Or pay a walk-in fee for a class that you select in your community. Something new and different promotes inspiration.*

#14

Walk an additional 1-2 miles that day. *The avid walker that I am, occasionally I will add to my miles that day. Adding increased exercise will help burn additional stress during the job search.*

#15

Plan a weekend get-a-way with a friend to rejuvenate yourself. Actually make reservations today. *Interestingly, taking a break from your job search actually makes you more productive in the job search. A weekend get-a-way can rejuvenate your mind, body and soul. I urge you to do so.*

#16

Have lunch with a former co-worker who is now working for a new company. *Here is a great networking opportunity, plus a time to catch up and reconnect. Regardless of whether it is a place you want to work, it's a chance to practice your networking.*

#17

Plan a few hours at a bookstore and find new books and tapes relating to your industry. *Rather than blow off the afternoon, head to the bookstore and immerse yourself in some new books. Most bookstores have sitting areas where you can read rather than buy the book and take it home (and maybe never read it). Recommend this over spending time on the internet. The idea is to get out of the house and away from your job search for an afternoon.*

#18

Develop a position you would like to have then find a company who will hear your proposal. *What is that dream job? What would be your job description, daily duties and responsibilities? Write it down and start brainstorming who would have such a position – regardless of whether it's open or not. Your proposal just may spark the desire to hire you for that position.*

#19

Write an ad for the ideal position you have in mind. *Play a dual role for a moment. Write an ad based on you being the employer and, the ideal person who can fill it. This exercise is from an employer's perspective of what they want and from an employee's perspective of what you have to offer when it's the ideal position for you.*

#20

Call companies that recently sent "thanks, but no thanks" letters and follow up regarding future positions. *Typically after receiving such a letter, the position has been filled. There are no guarantees that the person hired is the right fit and will stay. Things happen. By following up you let the company know that if things didn't work out with their selection, you're still interested. And, if anything else comes open that you may be better suited for, you welcome the opportunity to discuss further.*

#21

Go to a new networking function you've never attended before. *Take some business cards along with a smile and schmooze with some new folks. You just may be surprised at who you meet and the information or leads you obtain.*

#**22**

Have a picnic in the park with a friend and do a mock interview. *Here is a chance to have an inexpensive lunch and an opportunity to work on your interviewing skills at the same time. Make sure your friend is willing to give constructive feedback in helping you improve your interviewing techniques.*

#**23**

Practice conversations for salary negotiations. *Most importantly, practice the words: "what have you budgeted." Don't be too quick to give your salary requirements. Ask "what is their budget" or if the position is competitively priced. Do not give up your ability to negotiate by disclosing a salary range first.*

#24

Review your job search habits for new and fresh ideas and directions. *What else can you be doing? By week 6 or 8 (or 12 and beyond), review what you've accomplished so far, and identify any habits or patterns that may be putting you in a poor light with perspective employers. Think outside the box – get creative! Do something different to get different results!*

#25

Polish your 2-minute commercial for when you first meet someone. *The most commonly asked question is "tell me about yourself." In those 2 minutes, can you describe your strengths, expertise and what makes you stand out from the rest of the candidates?*

#26

Practice creative visualization and visualize yourself in your new position. *Visualization is a very powerful tool. If you are currently working and looking for a new job, visualize yourself going to your new job when you head off to work in the morning. If you are not working, as part of your job search, visualize yourself working at your new position and actually doing the work.*

#27

Research your contact file, weed out, update, and make a new appointment. *Throughout your job search, periodically go through your contacts. Who needs to be weeded out, updated or better yet, contacted? When making that contact, make a goal of scheduling an appointment.*

#**28**

Make a list of all the new businesses in your area and contact them for leads. *Business owners are great resources. Initially congratulate them on their success. Remember, networking is a two-way street. You are not asking for a job, you are contacting them regarding information or leads, and close the conversation by offering them something.*

29 Things To Do

#29

Plan tomorrow's activities! *Hopefully, you have a "To Do" list already started for tomorrow long before tomorrow comes. Planning ahead can keep you organized and achieve your goals more quickly.*

29 Things To Do

Good Luck in your job search!

ABOUT THE AUTHOR

Rosemary Augustine wrote her first book in 1995 titled *"Facing Changes In Employment"* and provides career advice to individuals ever since via coaching and her website: www.careeradvice.com. Her second book titled *"How to Live and Work Your Passion"* was released in 2000. Rosemary continues to be a model for "living your passion" and writes to inspire others to stay focused and follow their passion every day.

Rosemary discovered long ago that writing is her passion. When she relocated from her home in Denver, Colorado to NJ/PA area in 2001, something different happened besides a change of address. Rosemary embraced the culture of the northeast with a flair for creativity, which opened new directions for her as a writer. She maintains a daily writing practice as well as artistic endeavors including art journals, and acrylic painting.

By 2012, Rosemary blended 20 years of career coaching with creativity and self discovery. She released her third book titled: *365 Days of Creative Writing* (which offers journal prompts for every day of the year), and continues to value her creative spirit through writing. She has completed other written works including *Career Changers Guide to Finding the Work You Love*, *Secrets I Learned From Ordinary House Cats* and *Journal to a More Creative Self*.

Rosemary has numerous accolades awarded her since 1991 as an author, coach, speaker and trainer. Her proudest (besides her books) is her listing in Who's Who of American Women and Who's Who in the World (the 21st and 22nd Editions).

Formerly a licensed stock broker, before starting her writing and consulting business in 1991, Rosemary spent 20 years in Corporate America and another 20 years helping people transition out of corporate. She often jokes about how she ever survived the corporate rat-race, especially 20 years of it!

Today, Rosemary operates her life from a 2nd story flat in Berwyn, PA, and shares her home with two feisty felines – Ziggy and Zack. Visit her online:

www.**RosemaryAugustine**.com

www.**CareerAdvice**.com

. . .

www.ingramcontent.com/pod-product-compliance
Lightning Source LLC
Chambersburg PA
CBHW071803040426
42446CB00012B/2693